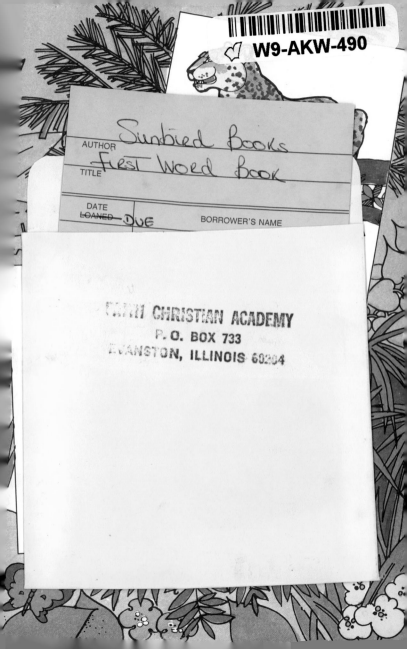

This series of books has been designed to stimulate talking and language development in young children.

Many of the pictures show things which the child will already know but several of the things he or she may not know. These will all provide topics for discussion and the opportunity for the child to learn something new.

If an adult looks at the books with the child and talks about the pictures, the value of the books will be increased. However, each book in the series is a delightful and interesting picture book in itself for every child.

The Sunbird: First Word Book is a picture dictionary for young children. This basic collection of words is about the child and his or her environment.

First edition

© LADYBIRD BOOKS LTD MCMLXXXII

Sunbird
first word book

compiled by
Seymour Kikine
designed and illustrated by
Hurlston Design Ltd

donkey

crayons

Ladybird Books Loughborough

bird

cat

cow

dog

donkey

duck

frog

goat

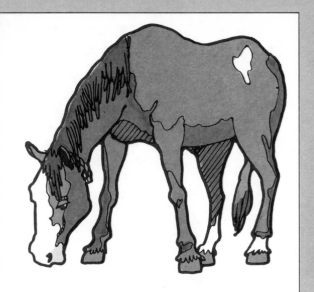

horse

mouse

rat

snake

zebra

giraffe

lion

elephant

leopard

hare

bee

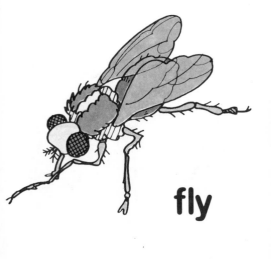

fly

beetle

butterfly

mosquito

grasshopper

spider

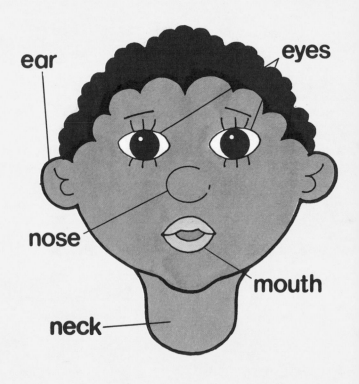

ear

eyes

nose

mouth

neck

head

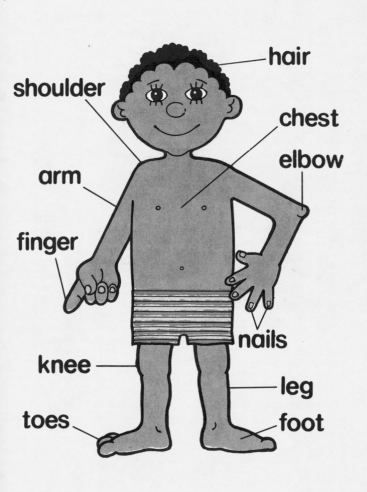

hair

shoulder

chest

elbow

arm

finger

nails

knee

leg

toes

foot

body

T-shirt shirt skirt

shorts

trousers

vest

18

socks

scarf

coat

shoes

dress

wrapper

19

grandmother

aunt

uncle

cousin

brother

grandfather

father

mother

sister

baby

pots

radio

kettle

jug

cooker

cupboard

mirror

basin

table

23

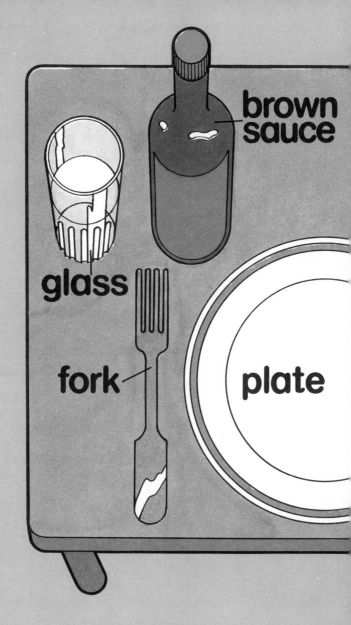

brown sauce

glass

fork

plate

pepper salt cup

saucer

knife

spoon

shower

doo

television

tap

mat

26

window

chair

bed

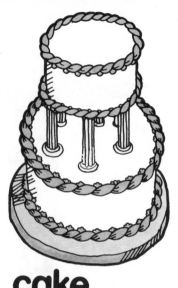

cake

milk

flour

28

beans

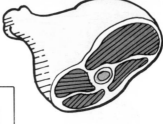

meat

fish

bread

carrots

cabbage

onion

potatoes

tomato

yams

melon

orange

pawpaw

pumpkin

banana

guava

pineapple

mango

coconut

schoolbag

book

pens

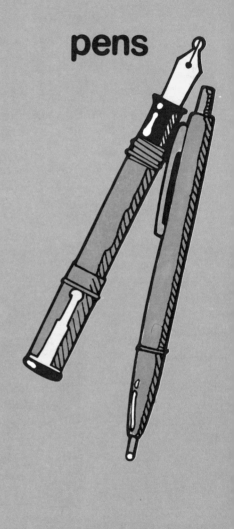

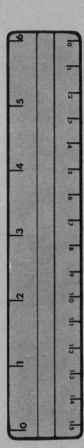

ruler

pencils

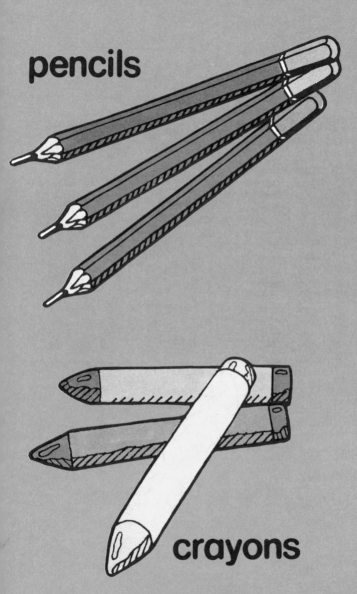

crayons

blackboard

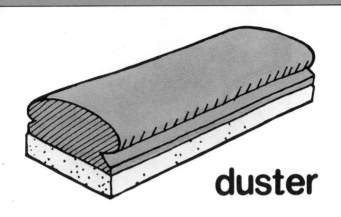

duster

chalk

nurse

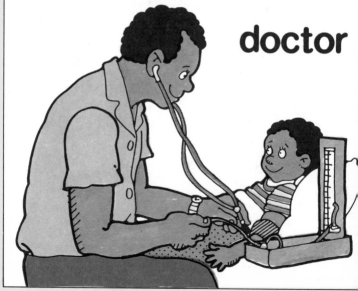

doctor

teacher

farmer

41

soldier

policeman

doll

car

bus

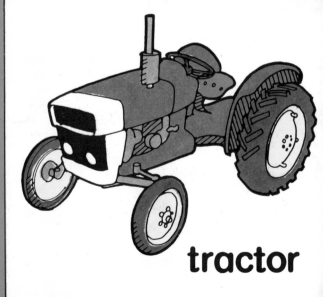

tractor

cards

ludo

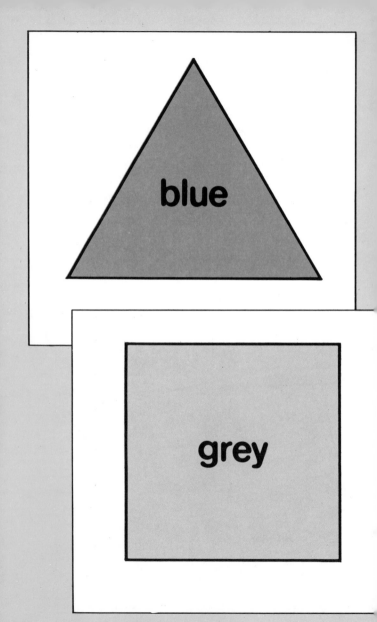

48

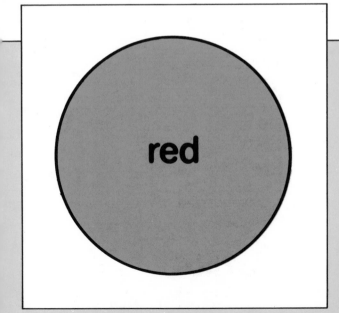

brown

red

black

green

white

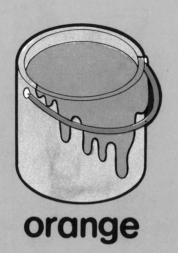

orange

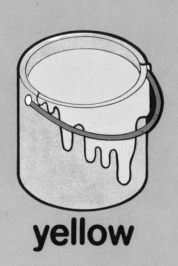

yellow

car

schoolbag

ball